D0777729

Through the Wilderness

Penn Mullin

High Noon Books
Novato, California

Cover Design and Interior Illustrations: Michael Cincotta

International Standard Book Number: 1-57128-118-5

10 09 08 07 06
2   1   0   9

A number of High Noon Books, like this *Trailblazers
Series*, are particularly appropriate as ancillary social stud-
ies materials. This may explain why the *Postcards Series*
and the *Four Corners Series* are so very popular. Write for
our free High Noon Books catalog that describes these and
many other titles.

Contents

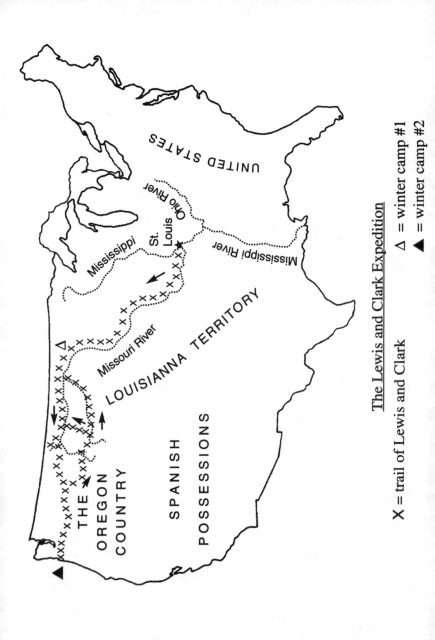

The Lewis and Clark Expedition

△ = winter camp #1
▲ = winter camp #2

X = trail of Lewis and Clark

CHAPTER 1

Orders from the President

It was a bright May morning in 1804. They were on their way at last! They had trained for five months. Now three boats set sail up the Missouri River. People cheered from shore.

Two army captains were the leaders. Their names were Meriwether Lewis and William Clark. Forty two men were with them. The two captains had orders from President Jefferson. Scout the Missouri River and the rivers beyond. Try to find a new trade route to the Pacific Ocean.

1

America had just bought a million square miles of land from France. It was called the Louisiana Territory. No one had yet explored it. All of this new land was west of St. Louis, Missouri. The captains and their men were starting their trip from this town.

They had two large wooden canoes. These were called *pirogues* (pee-ROWGES). They could be rowed or sailed. They also had a keelboat to carry men and supplies. It was 55 feet long. It had a sail and 20 oars. It also had a cabin in back for the captains. A small gun was placed on the front bow.

Tim Scott stood on the bow of this keelboat. He was 17 years old. Behind him the white sail was puffed out full. He looked ahead at the river. He felt full of excitement. What lay before them in the vast new lands? What steep mountains? What deep rivers? What strange animals? The President had lots of questions. It would be their job to bring him answers.

The President had picked fine leaders, Tim thought. He looked back at the boat's stern. The two captains stood there. Lewis with his dark hair, Clark with his red. They were both tall men. They looked strong and handsome in their uniforms. Lewis had his dog Scannon at his side.

Tim felt good about these two smart men. He knew he would follow them no matter where they led. And he would keep a journal, too, the way the captains did.

"We oarsmen get a day off," said John Mills. John was a crewman, too. "There's wind blowing!"

"It will be a long trip up the river. That current is strong," Tim said. "Our poor backs!"

"They say you're a top oarsman," laughed John. "I heard the captains saw you rowing one day. And they signed you up right away."

"I was lucky they came by," said Tim. "And I'm glad my pa let me go. He has to work the farm alone now. So how did you end up with Lewis and Clark?"

"I worked for Captain Clark in the army. He needed hunters on this trip. So here I am.

4

You better stay friends with me! I put food on the table!" John laughed.

"They say the land's full of elk, bear, buffalo. I just hope the Sioux (SUE) will let us pass through their lands," said Tim.

"There's danger ahead, that's for sure. Mountains to climb. Rivers full of sand bars and dead trees. Prairies full of Indians. It's a whole new country. And, just think, we're the first Americans to see it!" John said.

"I wonder how long till we see our homes once more." Tim looked back down the river. "I think it will be a long, long time."

CHAPTER 2

Up the Missouri!

Tim pulled hard on his oar. He was rowing one of the pirogues now. It was a hot August day. Sweat rolled down the men's bodies. All these summer days were the same. Rowing all day, camp and a hot meal on shore each night. Some days the river was only a few feet deep. Then they had to use poles to pull the boats along. Or get out and push the boats.

The prairies stretched out wide and flat on both sides of the river. They were filled with game. Horses were led along the banks for the hunters. John would jump on one and race off. One elk would feed the whole group.

"I'm ready for some buffalo meat," John told Tim. "We should see some soon. We're in the Sioux lands. The captains want to meet with the Sioux. That's why they set the prairie grass on fire each day. It was a signal."

"Look! The keelboat is pulling up to shore," said Tim. "I wonder what's up."

All three boats tied up on the bank. Then Tim and John saw why. A small group of Sioux Indians stood waiting. Behind them was their village of white tepees.

The captains greeted the Sioux chiefs. One

A small group of Sioux stood waiting.

man knew the Sioux language. He helped the two groups talk. Lewis spoke first. He told the Sioux that they were now under the care of the Great White Father. This father lived far away. He wished to set up trade with them. And he wanted them to live in peace with other tribes. The captains then brought out gifts for the Sioux chiefs.

"The big time was when Lewis pumped up his air rifle," Tim later wrote in his journal. "The Sioux just loved it when he shot it off."

That night Tim and John watched the Sioux braves dance. They tossed gifts of bells, beads, and knives to the dancers. The day had gone well. These Sioux would give no trouble on the trail. But would they keep their promise not to fight other tribes?

The boats were off again the next morning. And soon came the cry, "Buffalo!" The boats pulled to shore. The hunters raced off on horses. All Tim could see were buffalo. Thousands of them. They made a sound like thunder as they rushed by.

Shots rang out. Men dragged back huge chunks of buffalo meat. There was great joy and feasting that night. "It tastes better than elk," Tim said. "And I was sure tired of catfish!"

"I'll cut up some of this extra meat to jerk," said John. He cut thin strips to hang in the sun to dry. They would keep a long time.

"There go the captains, off to write in their journals," Tim told John. "They spend hours on them. They draw each plant and animal we find. And Clark makes maps."

"Just what President Jefferson wants. A list of all new things they see," said John.

"They will have a lot to send back to him next spring," laughed Tim. "Did you know they caught a barking squirrel?"

"The ones that live in those deep tunnels?" asked John. "They caught some live birds, too. Even toads! The boat that takes all these things back east will sink for sure!"

CHAPTER 3

The First Winter

"The days are colder now. The captains gave out warm shirts to each man today." Tim wrote this in his journal on October 1st. "Shallow water makes the trip hard. We use ropes and poles to move. We have passed Arikara (Air-a-CAR-a) towns. But no one was in them. Smallpox brought by white traders has killed so many. We hope to find a real village soon."

At last they did reach a village full of Arikaras. These Indians were not as warlike as the Sioux. They wished to hear all about their new White Father.

But it was soon time to push on. The plan was to spend the winter with the Mandan Indians up the river. They must hurry. Now men began to get sick from the cold.

"We're lucky to have Lewis here! He can cure anything," said Tim. "Did you see how he fixed Clark's sore neck? He wrapped a hot stone in flannel. Then he put it on Clark's neck. Cured him right up!"

"You would think he was a real doctor," laughed John. "What an amazing man!"

"I just hope none of us gets smallpox, though," said Tim. "Even the captains have no cure for that."

At the end of October they reached the Mandan villages. Their homes were covered with earth. They were built on cliffs above the river. The men began to work on cabins for a winter camp.

"Our Fort Mandan is ready at last! Now winter can come. We will be warm in our eight cabins," Tim wrote. "It has been five months since I left home. And we have come 1,600 miles!"

The captains worked hard through the bitter cold winter. They drew up maps. They wrote in their journals. They learned all they could about Indian tribes in the lands ahead. Both men spent a lot of time with the sick.

"The Mandans have heard what good doctors we have," Tim told John. "They are lined up to see the captains, too! Last week Lewis gave the young girl Sacajawea (Sack-a-juh-WE-a) a drink made from a rattlesnake's rattle," said Tim. "They say it saved her life."

"She is the wife of the man who interprets for us. Right?" asked John.

"Yes. She is a Shoshone (Sho-SHOW-nee). She was captured away from her tribe," Tim said. "The captains say she can help us with the Shoshones. We need horses from them to cross the mountains."

"She and her baby will come with us?"

John stared at Tim. "That is foolish!"

"The captains say she knows the lands where we're going," said Tim.

"This trip is no place for a woman and baby," John said. "You wait and see."

The last part of winter was spent packing nine boxes. They would be sent back to the President. They held hundreds of things. There were plants, bones, live birds, even a prairie dog! Plus the captains' lists and maps.

The keelboat left on April 7. It was headed for the East with its rich load. The rest of the group set out for the unknown West that same day.

"I had a strange feeling when I saw the men leave for the East," Tim wrote. "A small part of me wished to go back with them. But a larger part wished to stay. I don't want to miss out on what's ahead for us!"

The group now used the two pirogues and six new canoes. Three people had joined the group. They were Sacajawea, her husband, and their baby.

"I thought Lewis might leave Scannon behind," John laughed. "The Mandans loved him. They offered three beaver pelts for him!"

"Lewis would never give up his dog," said Tim.

Spring was near. Flowers bloomed on the prairies now. And the mosquitoes came. "There is no escape from them," Tim wrote. "I fear I will go mad!"

The boats sailed on up the river. All of a sudden a high wind came up! One of the pirogues began to rock. Medicines, lists, and many lives were nearly lost in the river.

Soon they came to the mouth of the Yellowstone River. "It is a time to be merry," Tim wrote. "We have come this far! We had a feast of wild turkey and trout. We sang and danced to Al's fiddle. We all feel full of hope. We are closer to the end of the trail."

CHAPTER 4

Close Calls

They were in grizzly country now. The huge bears were all along the river. The men knew they were much more wild than bears back east.

"I bet one would weigh 600 pounds!" John said. He was cleaning his gun. "I'd better be ready if I see one when we go to hunt elk. Clark says these bears are hard to kill. They just keep coming. And our rifles take so long to reload."

"Watch out!" laughed Tim. "Stay out of berry patches where the bears might be!"

"I sure will!" John called back. He and five men set out on foot along the river bank.

All of a sudden they came upon a huge grizzly! John and three others fired at him. No one missed. The angry bear charged. The four bullets had not been enough!

The next two men fired. Still the bear came. He had not slowed up. John knew they had no time to reload. They had to run for their lives! Two men jumped into a canoe. John and three others hid in some bushes to reload. They could hear the huge beast pant as it searched for them. It tore through the brush. Closer, closer! John made a run for the cliff with the bear at his heels. He had to jump – or else! Over he went,

All of a sudden they came upon a huge grizzly.

20 feet down into the river! Just then a man on shore shot the grizzly.

"Eight bullets went through its body! Can you believe that?" John told Tim later.

The spring days passed quickly. Now they came into hilly, rough land. There was talk of the Rocky Mountains. And there they were on May 26. "They look so high," wrote Tim. "And they lie between us and the Pacific!"

The group pushed on up the Missouri River. They camped each night on shore. They kept extra guards to watch for grizzlies! But the guards did not expect a buffalo! He came charging straight for the captains' tent.

"What the blazes!" Tim woke up. A huge

dark shape raced towards him. Tim froze. Was it a grizzly? All of a sudden Scannon barked loudly. The huge buffalo turned. It raced off into the night. It had missed the sleepers by inches!

"John, you're our hunter," Tim laughed. "And you never even woke up! We're lucky Scannon did!"

A few days later they came to a sudden fork in the river. It turned into two large streams. One was muddy brown. One was clear. Which one was the Missouri? The captains chose the clear south fork. It looked as if came from the mountains.

"But we men chose the north fork. It was

brown like the Missouri," Tim wrote in his journal. "Each captain led a group up one of the forks. When they got back, they were still sure of the south fork. But we did not take that fork. Not yet. The Indians told Lewis there were big waterfalls on the Missouri. So he went on by land to find them. We are now with Clark. We are going up the river. I hope Lewis is safe."

Lewis and his men heard the roar of the falls from far away. Spray rose like smoke high in the air. The falls were 300 yards wide and 90 feet high! The Indians had been right. This fork was the Missouri.

The mountains were close now. The captains would need horses and guides. They hoped to meet up with the Shoshones soon. Lewis had American flags flown on the canoes. This was to show that they came in peace.

Sacajawea now knew the land. She had grown up near there. She said the river would divide into three branches. And it did.

One branch seemed to lead into the mountains. So they took it. The rapids were fast. Tim wrote, "Our canoes must be poled or dragged now. Our feet are bloody and sore from the sharp stones. Many are sick with fevers and boils. Both captains, too. Mosquitoes will not stop. But we keep going. Where are the Shoshones? We must cross the mountains before snow comes!"

CHAPTER 5

On to the Pacific!

Lewis set off with three men to look for Shoshones. They took an Indian trail through a high mountain pass. Then Lewis found a stream. Its water ran towards the Pacific. This meant they had now left the United States. This was Oregon country. England and America both wanted this land. It was rich in furs.

Lewis met up with Shoshones at last. He made signs of peace. He had learned them from Sacajawea. Then he and his men were taken to the Shoshone camp. There they were smeared with paint in welcome. Lewis smoked the peace pipe with their chief. Then he gave out gifts to all. Horses would be given to them. The future looked bright.

"Sacajawea was full of joy. It was so good to see her Shoshone people again," Tim wrote. "She ran to one woman and hugged her. They had been friends as girls."

Sacajawea was called in. She was needed to interpret for the captains and the chief. John was nearby as a guard. He saw it all.

"She came in and sat down. But then she jumped up and ran over to the chief," John told Tim. "She saw he was her *brother*! We were all amazed. She had thought she would never see him again."

It was the end of August. The captains and their group said goodbye to the Shoshones. They now had horses and guides. And the Shoshones were their friends. But winter seemed close at hand. Snow and sleet came down as they pushed through the mountains. Horses slipped and fell on the ice. There was no game to shoot on the trail now. They had to kill their own colts for food.

"I wonder if we'll make it to the Pacific," Tim wrote. "We are all so tired, sick, hungry. It would be easy to just lie down in the snow right here and stop."

But the next day Tim watched Clark take John and others off to search for game. The captains would not let their men die here. Not when they had come this far. Clark soon found some Indians. They were friendly. They gave them dried salmon and some roots to eat. But the whole group got ill from eating the roots.

"I will starve rather than eat more roots," John told Tim. "Even Lewis is sick!"

Those not sick carved out dugout canoes. The group then left the horses with the Indians and set off down the Clearwater River. At last they reached the Columbia River!

"We have found it! This river flows to the Pacific! We all have hope again. And I am not still sick from the roots," Tim wrote.

Now the canoes raced through deep canyons. Some cliffs were as high as 3,000 feet! Canoes were tossed onto rocks and turned over. The men had to carry them around the worst rapids and falls. Next the river narrowed. It was full of huge rocks. The canoes had to slide through narrow slots.

"I thought we were all lost. We would be smashed to bits. But we slid through. Indians watched us from the cliff tops," Tim wrote that night. "And now we look up at a high snowy peak above us."

The men fixed their canoes and set off again. They could make 30 miles a day now. On they raced towards the Pacific. Thick fog rolled in. Now they could feel the pull of the tides. At last came the big day. A shout went up from the lead canoe. The ocean! They could hear the waves pound on the shore. "Great joy in camp," Tim wrote on November 7. "We have reached the Pacific! Clark says we have come 4,142 miles from the mouth of the Missouri!"

CHAPTER 6

A Fort at the Coast – Winter 1804-5

But there was still a ways to go. The river was six miles wide. It was very rough. High waves rolled in from the ocean. Cold rain pounded down on the seasick men. Huge fallen trees drifted towards their canoes. The men tried to camp near the mouth of the river. The land was damp. High tides swept through their camps. They were hungry for meat. There was no game.

"I won't eat that pounded fish again," John told Tim. "It is moldy. We're all sick. When will we see some elk?"

The next day John got his wish. And it was he who shot the huge elk. It fed the whole camp. The men's spirits rose with this feast.

"Lewis has found us a place for our winter fort," Tim wrote in his journal on December 1st. "It's not far from here. It's on a small river. I think it will be a good spot. It's up in the fir trees, safe from the tides. We start work on it soon. How I wish this rain would stop! Our clothes never dry. My leather pants are rotted. I hope we find more elk. Their hide makes the best clothes."

The winter fort was just three miles from the ocean. The captains hoped to meet a ship from the east coast. They needed to buy supplies from her.

Work began on the log fort. It was to be 50 feet square. The cabins would be built inside its walls. There was a pair of gates on one side. The men named it Fort Clatsop for Indians who had been kind to them. They were moved in by Christmas, 1805.

"What a day of joy!" wrote Tim. "We are snug and dry in our fort. The captains gave us all gifts. A handkerchief for me. Tobacco for John. I cannot help but think of home today. I wish I could tell Ma and Pa I am safe. Will I be home next year on this day?"

The new year began with big news. A

Work began on the log fort.

whale had washed up on the beach! The captains named men to go out and bring back blubber. Sacajawea announced that she wanted to go, too. She had come too far to miss seeing this great fish. So she went off with the men. Her son was on her back.

"She kept right up with us," John told Tim. "I do like her spirit. She was so sad when we reached the whale. It was only a skeleton. The Indians had been there first. But she helped Clark make a deal with them. He then bought blubber and whale oil for us!"

It was a long winter of rain. John gained fame as the best shot in camp. In one day he killed seven elk. Now there was plenty to eat.

The men worked hard tanning the elk hides. They would need new clothes for the trip home in the spring.

"The captains are always at work on their maps and notebooks," Tim wrote. "The President will be pleased with them. They write so much. I wish my journals were as good. I wonder if people will want to read mine some day."

By early spring the elk had moved off. No ship had come with supplies. It was time to start the long trip home. The captains gave their fort to one of the Clatsop chiefs.

In late March they set out by canoe up the Columbia River. It was an easier trip this time.

The men bought horses from the Indians. They portaged around the falls. Later they sold their canoes or used them for firewood.

Soon they were in the lands of the Nez Perces (Nay-pear-SAY) (pierced nose). Chiefs from this friendly tribe met with the captains. They heard how the United States wished peace and trade with them. Sacajawea helped as interpreter.

The Nez Perces knew of the captains' great skill in curing the sick. Now they brought in a chief who could not move at all. Clark tried his famous sweat bath in a deep pit. It cured him in no time.

In June the Nez Perces led them back

across the Bitterroot Mountains. "Our trail is far easier now," wrote Tim. "And we need not kill our horses for food. John supplies us!"

It was now early July. The captains wanted to see more new land as they moved east. Lewis would scout the Marias River area. Clark would go east through the Yellowstone River lands. They would meet where the Missouri and Yellowstone join.

"I feel it's unwise to split up," Tim wrote. "But the captains know best. John stays with Clark. I go with Lewis. We will have much to tell each other when we next meet!"

CHAPTER 7

Where the Rivers Join

Clark's group reached the meeting place first on August 3. But the mosquitoes were so bad that they could not camp there. Sacajawea's son was very ill from the bites. So they moved downstream a ways.

Clark left a note for Lewis. But it was nine days before the two groups met at last. There were cheers and shouts of joy. But where was Lewis himself?

"We were scared when we didn't see him,"

John told Tim. "Then there he was lying down in the canoe! He had been shot?"

"By one of our own hunters. It was a big mistake. Lewis has a bad fever. But Clark has fixed the wound up fine," said Tim. The two friends sat on the river bank after supper.

"Where do we start? There's so much to tell," said John. "The Yellowstone has great broad valleys. What beauty! Sacajawea guided us there. She had been there as a child. You know, I was so wrong about her. What a strong, brave woman! Did you hear Clark wants to adopt her son? He has grown so fond of the boy."

"Our captains are fine men. It was great to

be with Lewis these past weeks. What a leader
he is!" said Tim.

"I heard there was trouble with the
Blackfeet," John asked.

"They ran off with some guns and horses.
But we fought hard. They are not to be trusted.
Lewis was right," Tim said. "It is good to have
us all together again."

"But not for long. I hear we'll make St.
Louis by September!" said John. "What will
you do then?"

"Go home and help Pa with the farm I
guess," Tim laughed. "I bet he'll be surprised
I'm still alive. Two years without a word from
me. What about you, John? Have you made up

your mind? Will you stay in the army?"

"Clark asked me to stay with him when we get back," John smiled. "Who knows where we will be? But I'm honored."

"It should be a smooth trip back from now on. We have the current with us," said Tim. "I know the captains want to stop at the Mandans. They hope a chief will come with them to Washington."

"Perhaps one will. The country will be changed from now on. The captains have opened up a whole new world out here." John stood up and stretched. "Well, I must be off to sleep. If the bugs will let me! I guess you'll write in that journal first. I wish I'd kept one.

Well, g'night, Tim. Glad we're both back safe."
John walked off into the night.

Tim took out his journal. There was still enough light left to write. "We are just a few weeks from home now. And I have such strange thoughts. I know I'll go back and help Pa. Life will still be the same there. But *I* have changed. I am not that same boy who left home two years ago. The world seems so large to me now. I'm glad the captains saw me rowing that day. I was lucky."